Laurent La Gamba

Works on canvas
Portraits and Self-portraits

1998 - 2001

Laurent La Gamba
Works on canvas
Portraits and Self-portraits
1998 - 2001

LAURENT LA GAMBA

WORKS ON CANVAS
PORTRAITS AND SELF-PORTRAITS
1998 - 2001

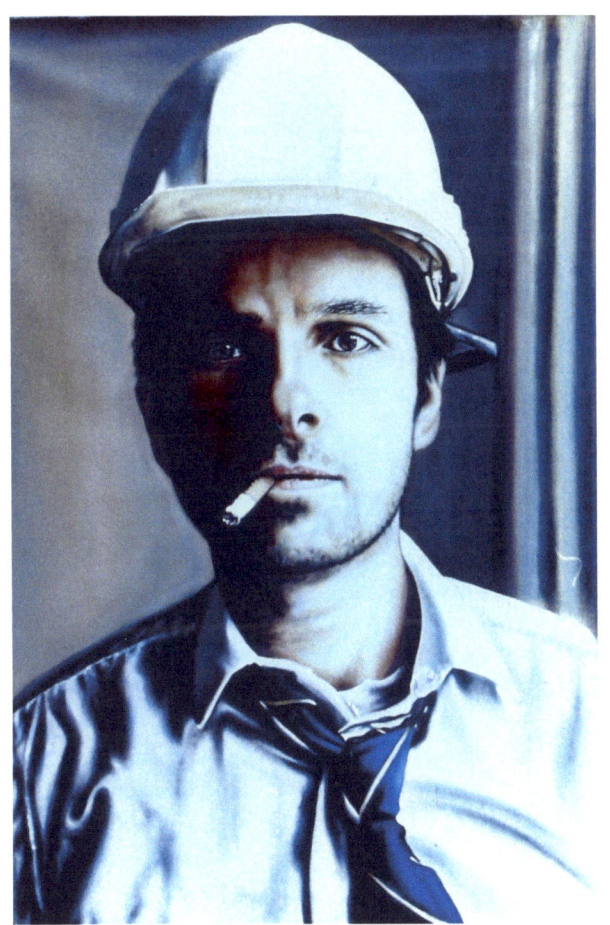

Matisse Avenue Books

Cover: *Self-portrait as the Team Rocket, 200 x 150 cm, 2001, acrylic on canvas.*

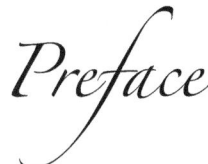

Preface

In 2003, the artist explains: "The main influence I received from Lacan's "Purloined Letter" in which the sentence: "The style is the man himself" is replaced by "The style is the man we are talking/turning to...", meaning that the ego is like an empty skin and needs to be filled by the echo received from the message sent to the others. This answer is sometimes given by the appearance of the person and the ego's development is aligned with the level of the other's desire.

Laurent La Gamba's portraits and self-portraits series try to visualize the phenomenon of this echo-process. The object of the gaze, is playing its part as this sexual travesty through masquerade (make-up) that we didn't acknowledge was Lacan's reference to display.

The masquerade (the "mask-erade") takes place in the symbolic register. The reflective surface of the self-portrait's eye is a kind of metaphorical way of invoking the reflection of the spectator's gaze calling up the notion of the mirror phase.

La Gamba is playing with consumer emblems and marketing patterns (the Disneyland patterns for example) to draw a ironical point of identification with the character photographed. For the artist the self-portrait genre is an instrument, a medium, a rhetoric, delivering a compete range of self-representation. It's a shift.

La Gamba tries to explore the subversive potential in society to produce satirical canvases. It's a symbiosis of precarious ego fictions and pictorial discovery of the fundamental instability of the self.

The self-portraiture manufactured genre can sneak itself into fragmentary disruptive presences. The portraits and self-portraits melodramatize and reimagine the artist own physiognomy displaying a kind of modern existential heroism turned into absurdity or sometimes social and political critic.

The figure as a neurotic and obsessive pattern is absolutely predominant in all his work. His interests lie in showing how identification processes can go both ways, from one extreme to the other and sometimes how different identities can coexist for some time before a path is chosen. His work has aimed at showing this alluring and inherently human schizophrenia (see for example the painting Raphrent, contraction for Raphael and Laurent)

Same thing in the temptation of using the same cigarette each time which can be seen under two lights: one, there is the will to play with this virtual element of identification (He does not smoke, therefore the viewer has not only no idea who he is but also it means that he can create any idea of the artist's ostentatious "image"), and two, it echoes back to this self-portrait series in which La Gamba always use this cigarette as a pattern from one painting to the next.

For the artist the self-portraiture posture modifies the man's desire for the female/woman's masquerade, and attempts to visualize the body/figure in the process of negotiating the aggressive identification process with his masculine ideal.

Claire Duane

Laurent La Gamba

Works on canvas
Portraits and Self-portraits

1998 - 2001

Self-portrait with rasor and camera, 2000, acrylic on canvas, 190 x 150 cm

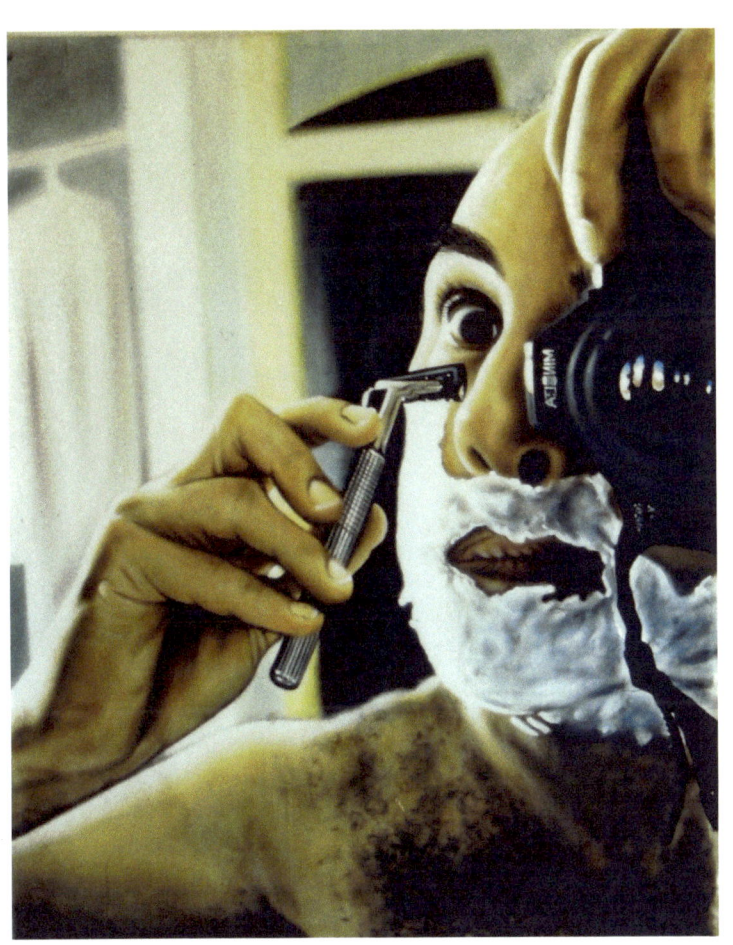

Self-portrait as The Team Rocket, 2000, acrylic on canvas, 200 x 150 cm

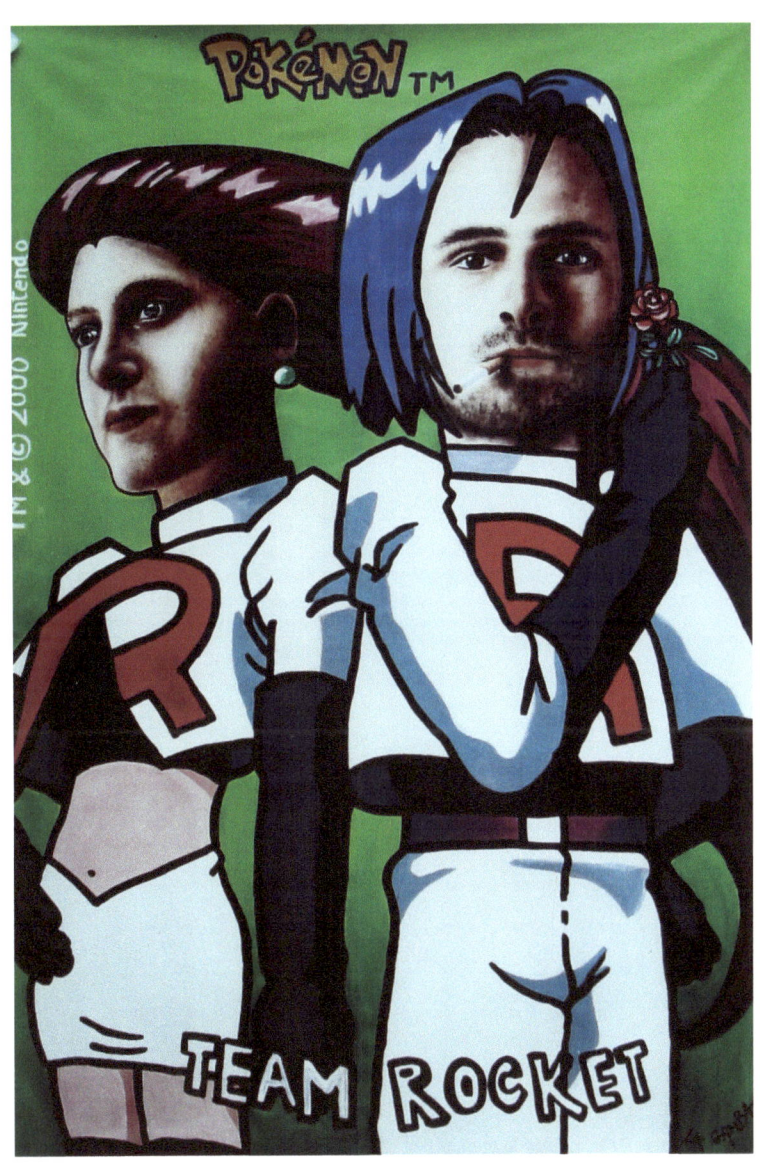

Self-portrait as an architect, 1999, acrylic on canvas, 220 x 150 cm

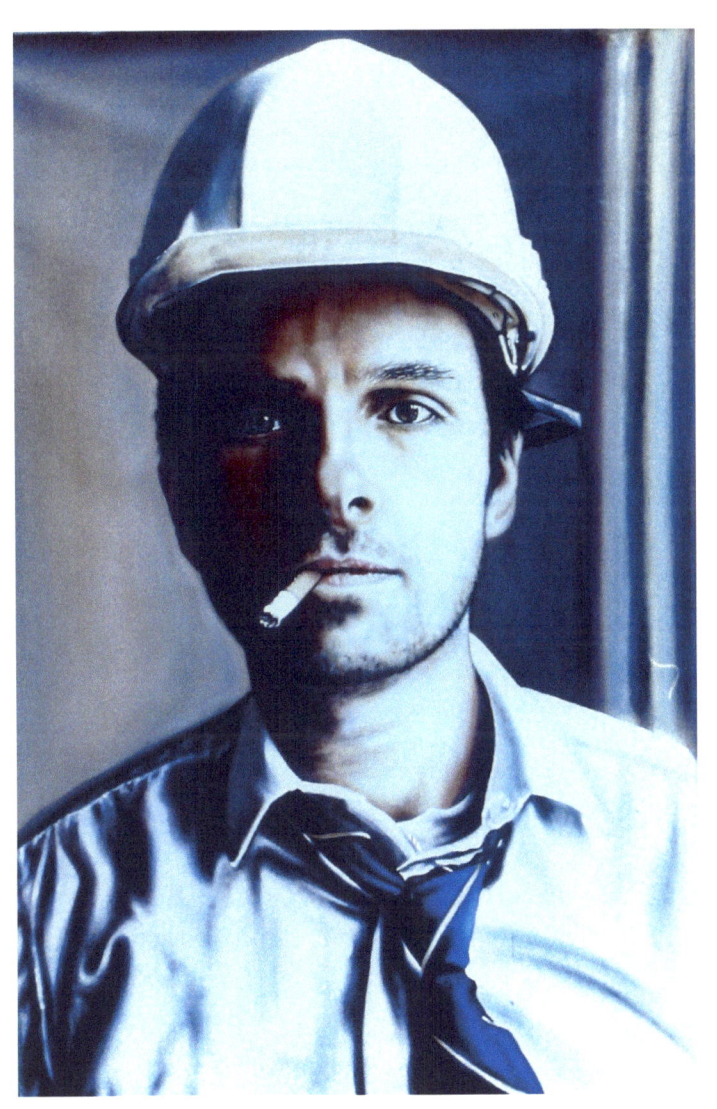

Self-portrait as a portion of French fries, 2000, acrylic on canvas, 210 x 140 cm

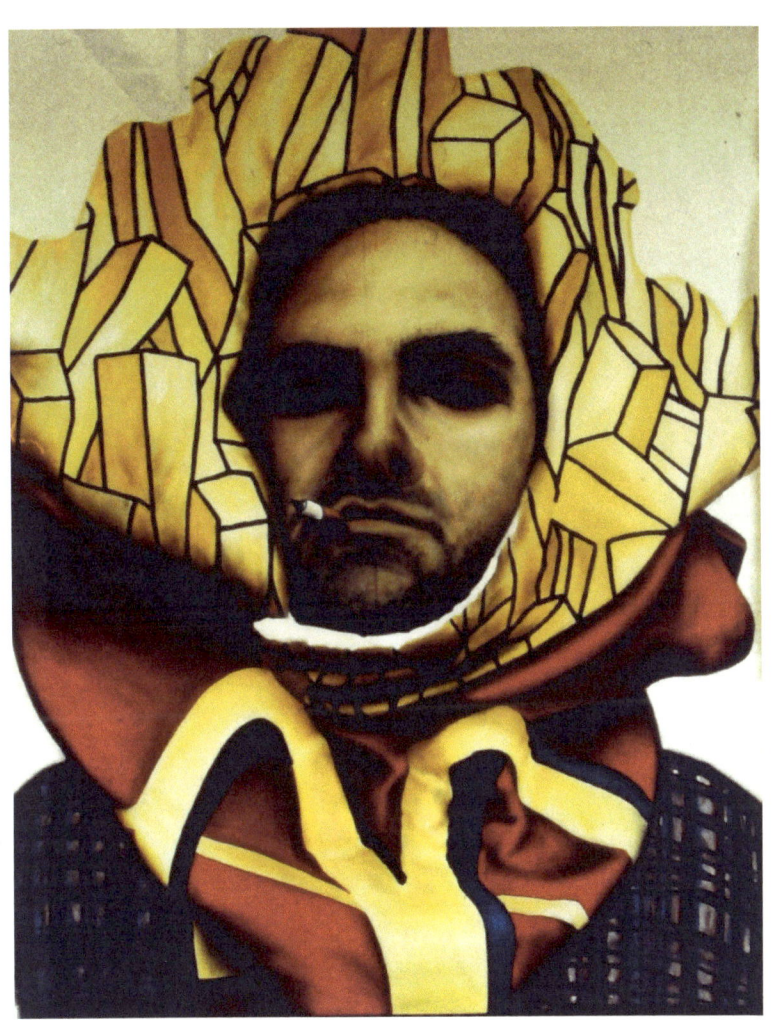

Self-portrait as an Air France stewardess, 2000, acrylic on canvas, 200 x 150 cm

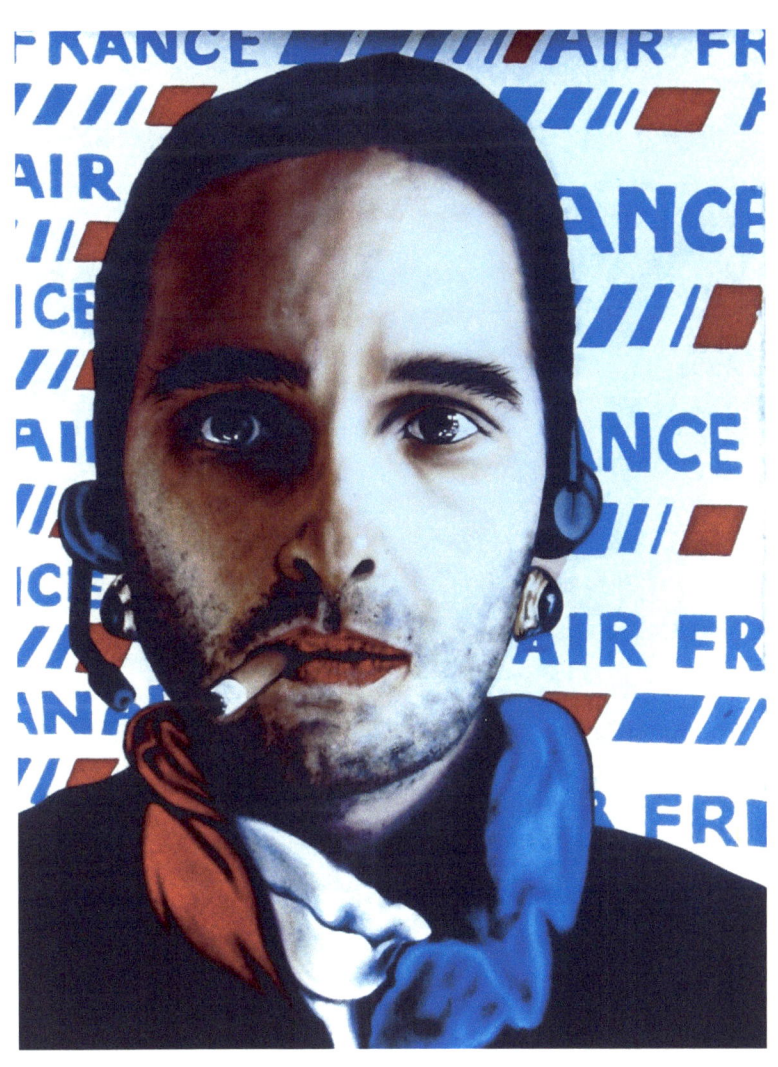

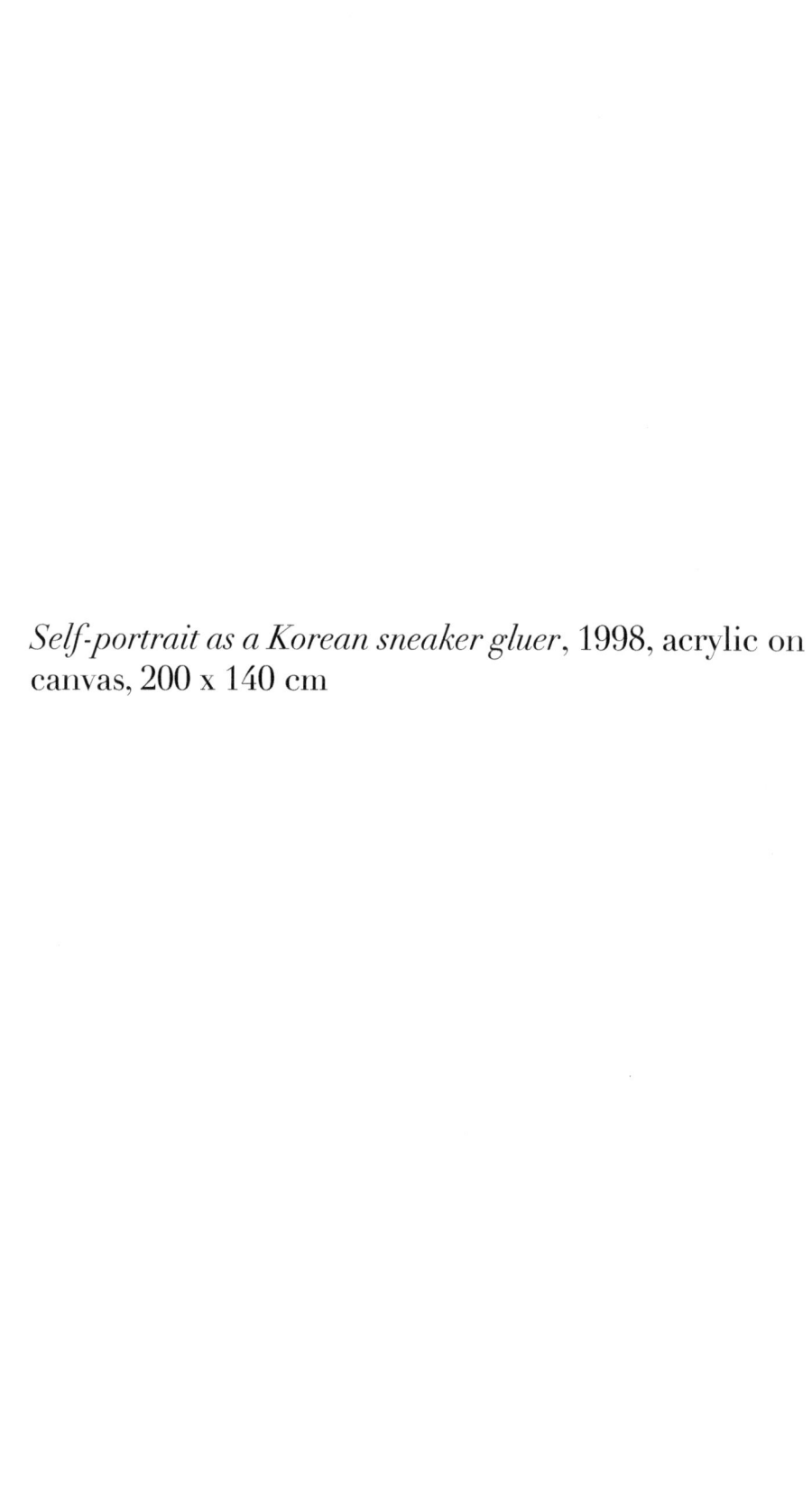

Self-portrait as a Korean sneaker gluer, 1998, acrylic on canvas, 200 x 140 cm

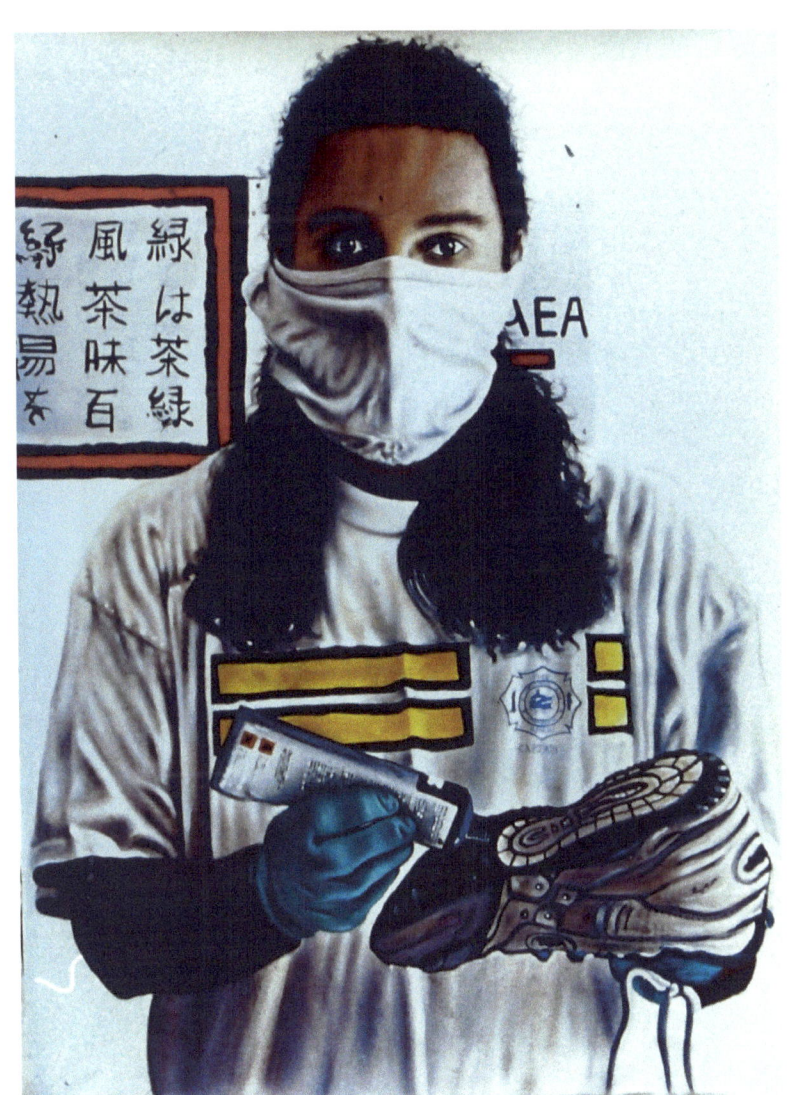

Self-portrait as a Playmobil, 2000, acrylic on canvas, 190 x 150 cm

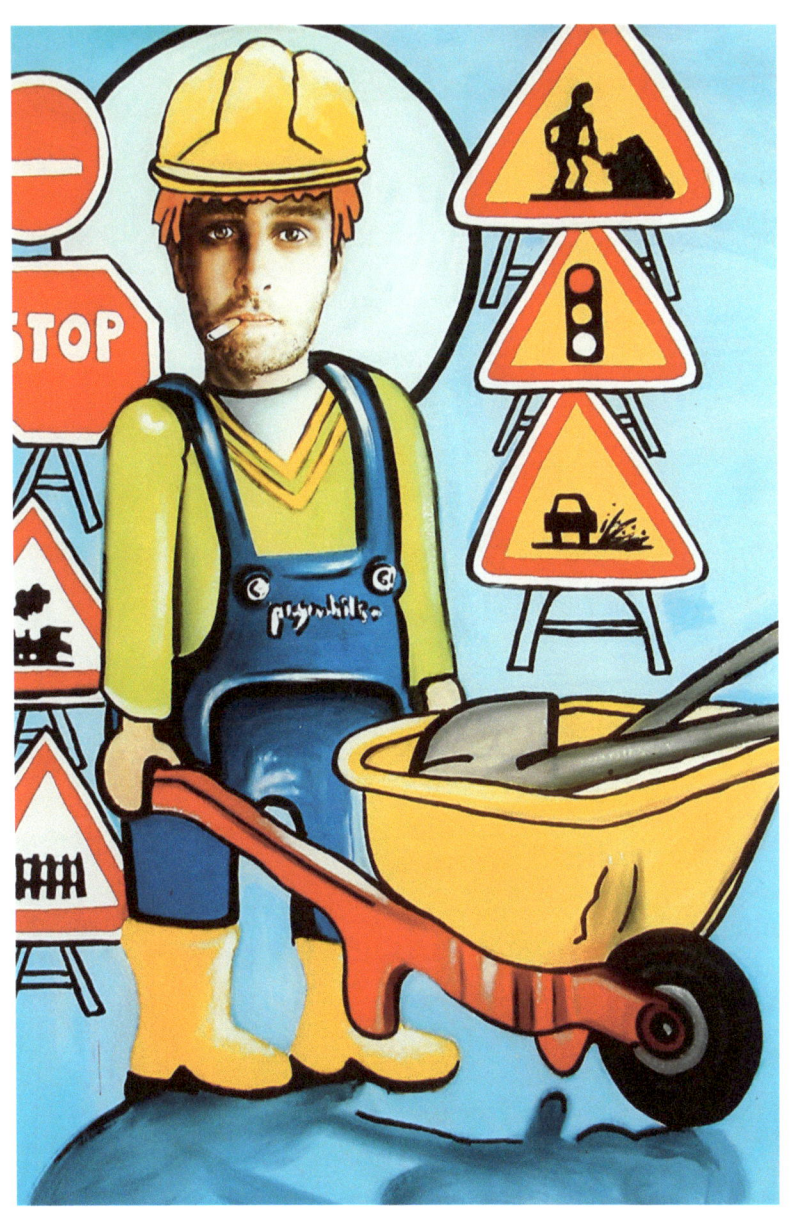

Smoking but not smiling Dalaï-lama, 2000, acrylic on canvas, 190 x 150 cm

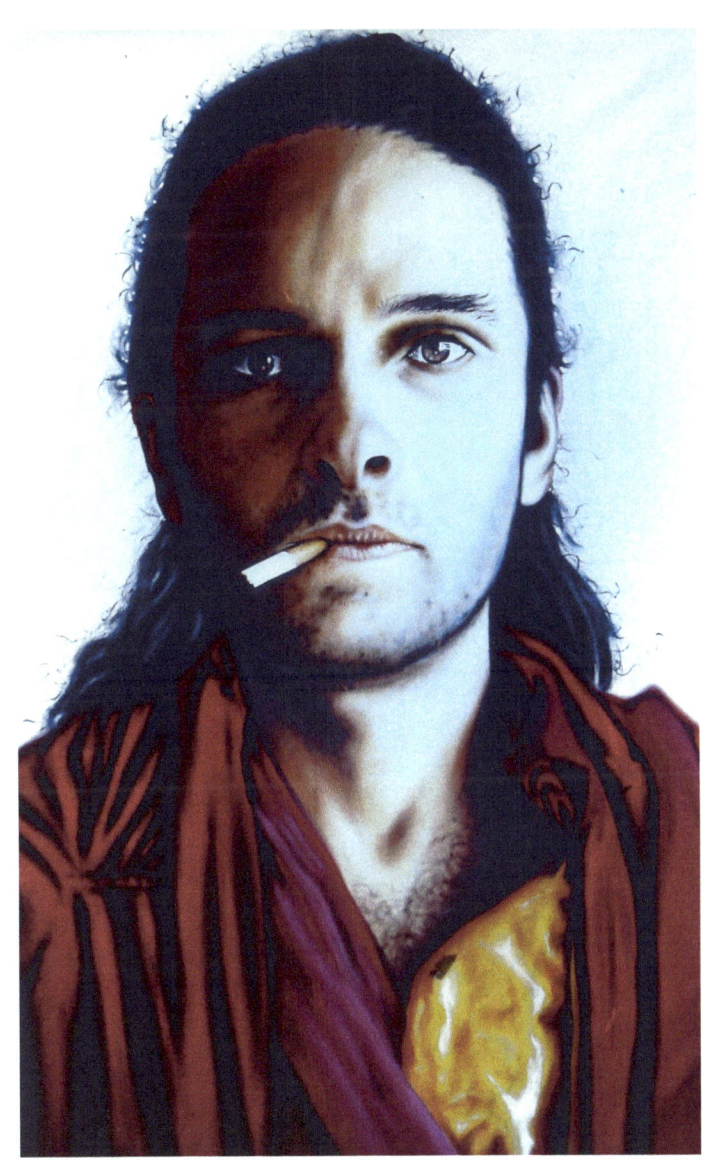

Self-portrait as a Pokemon, 1999, acrylic on canvas, 180 x 150 cm

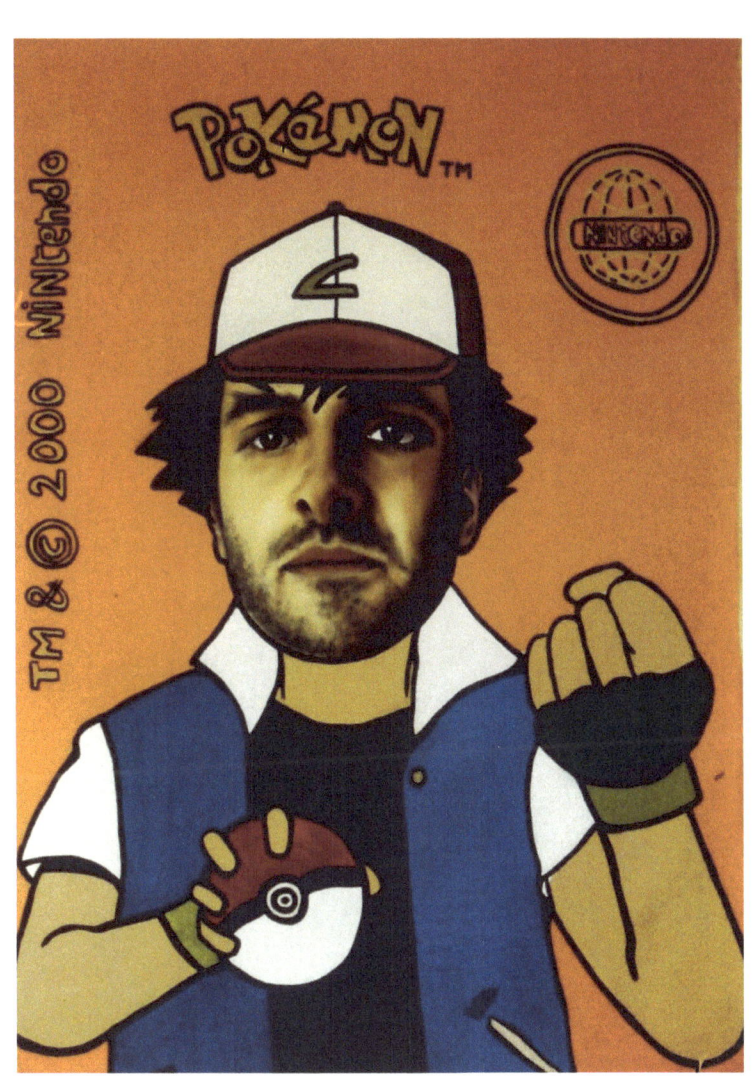

Self-portrait as a Mc Donald´s bride, 2001, acrylic on canvas, 150 x 180 cm

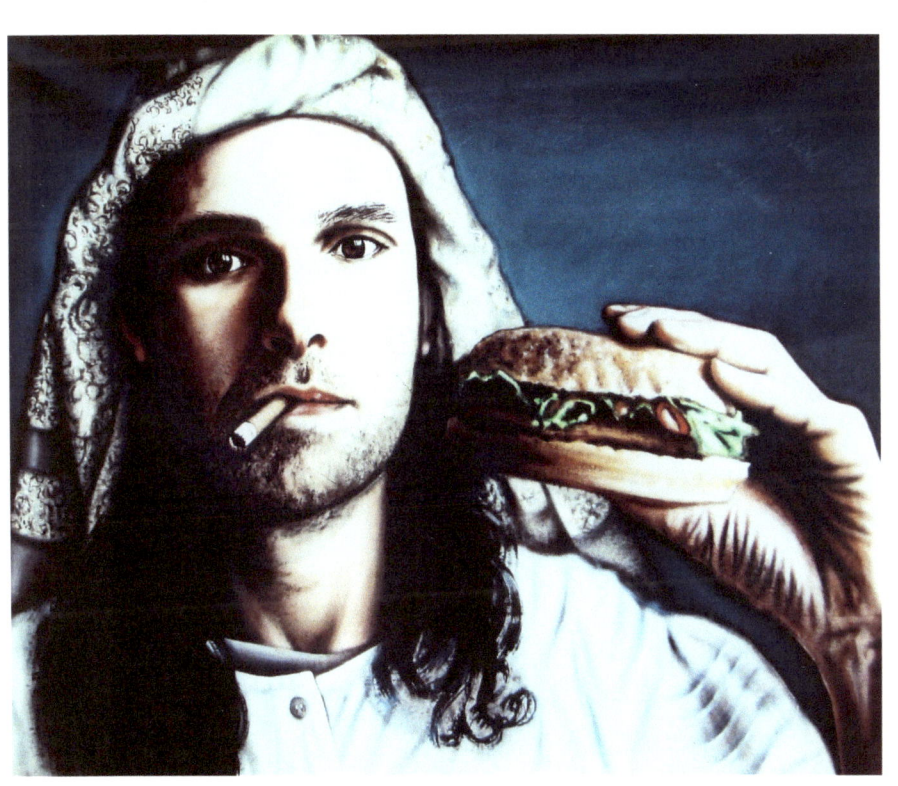

Self-portrait as Al the Builder, 2000, acrylic on canvas, 190 x 190 cm

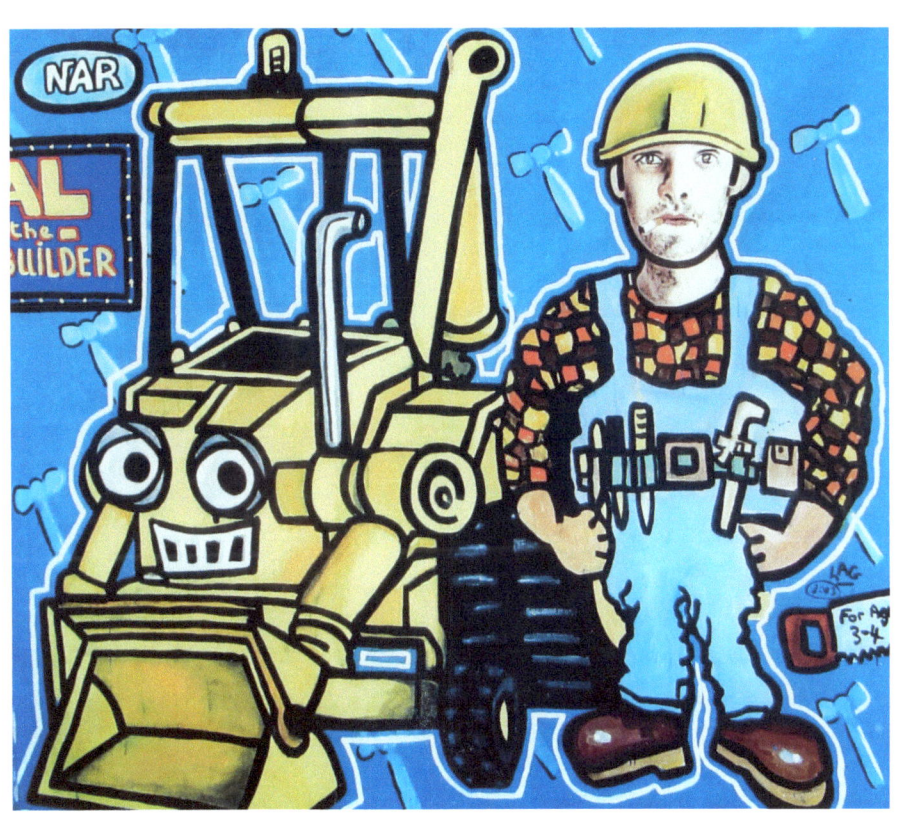

Working for the United States Postal Service, 2001, acrylic on canvas, 190 x 150 cm

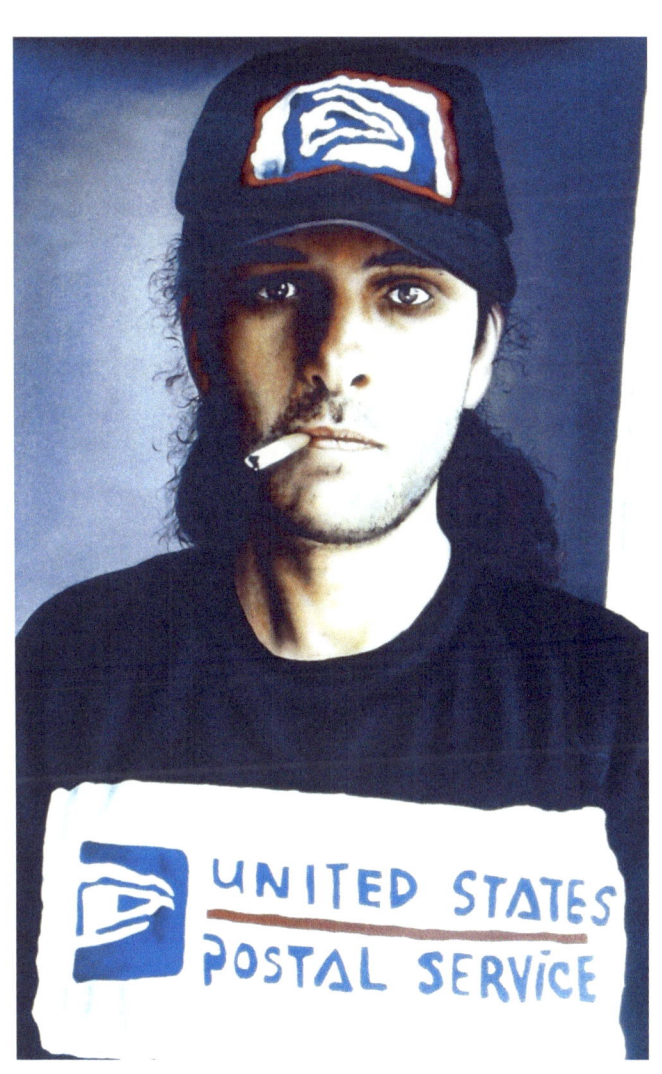

Self-portrait with paint-brush and cigarette, 2000, acrylic on canvas, 203 x 151 cm

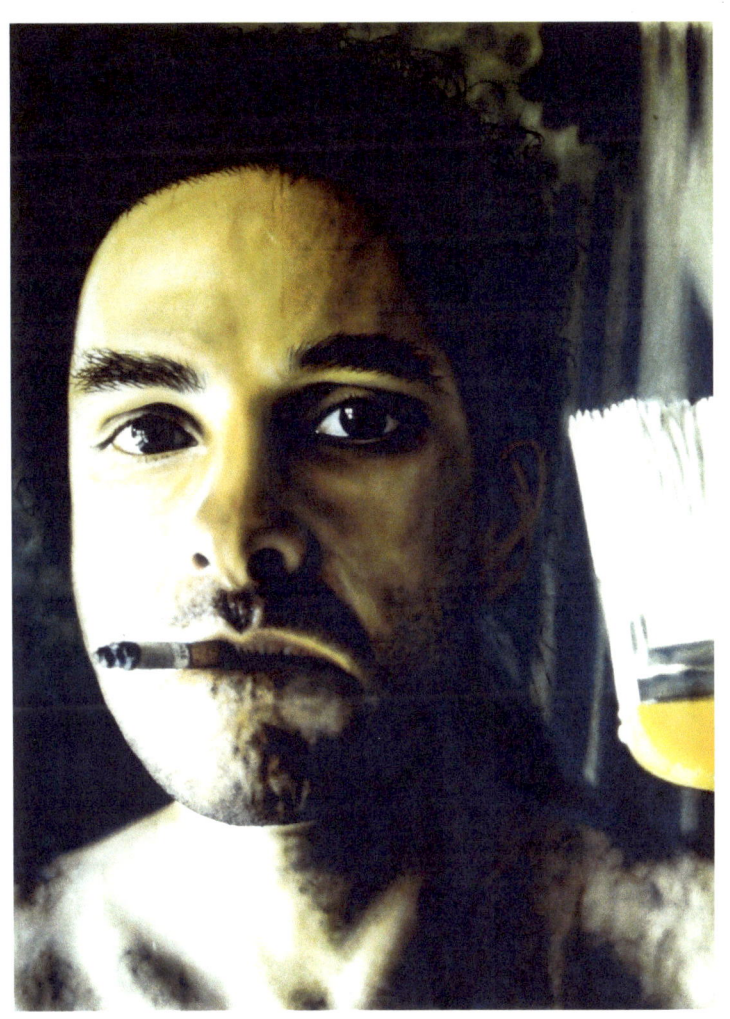

Self-portrait as a gang leader with 101 Damatian´s bandana, 2001, acrylic on canvas, 190 x 150 cm

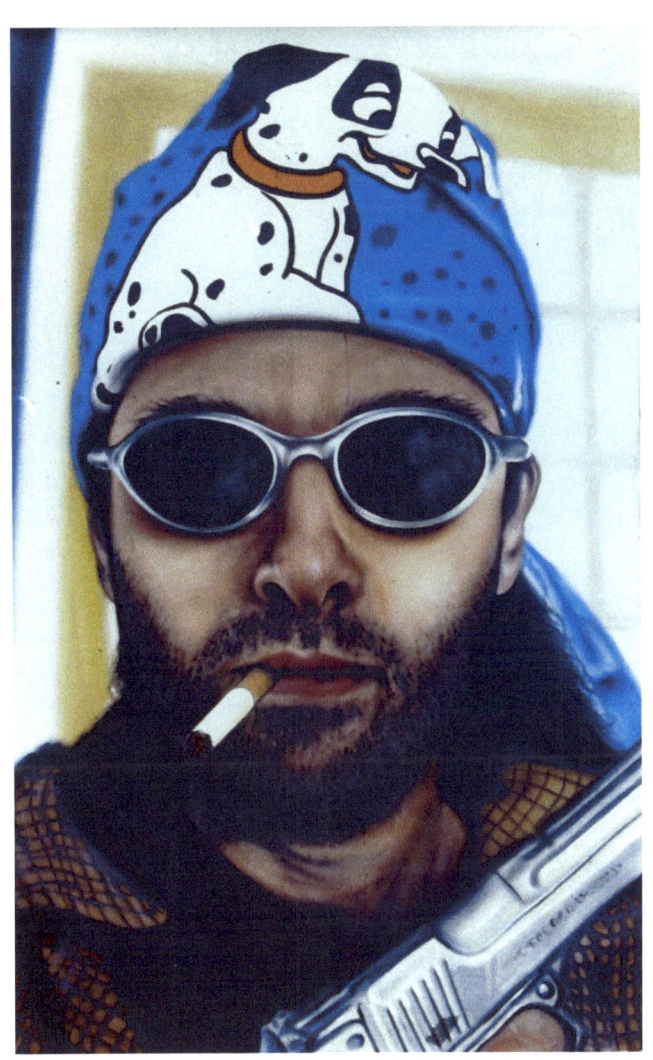

Self-portrait with toothbrush and camera, 2000, acrylic on canvas, 200 x 140 cm

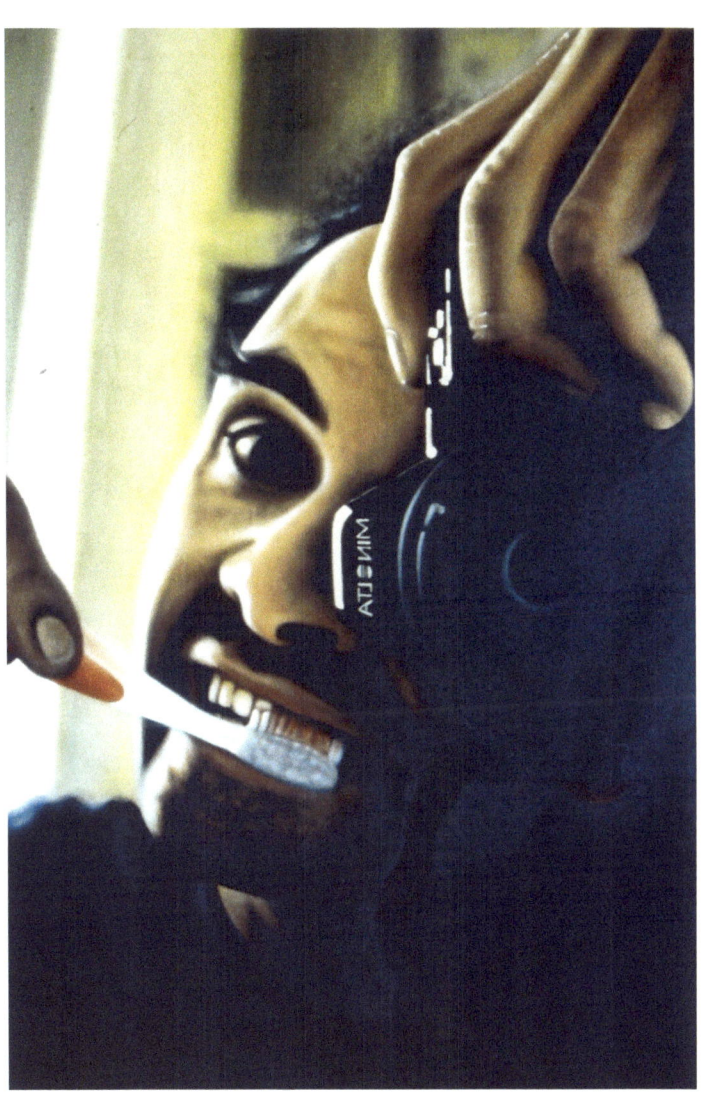

Choosing an identity: the Lama-Geisha, 2000, acrylic on canvas, 190 x 150 cm

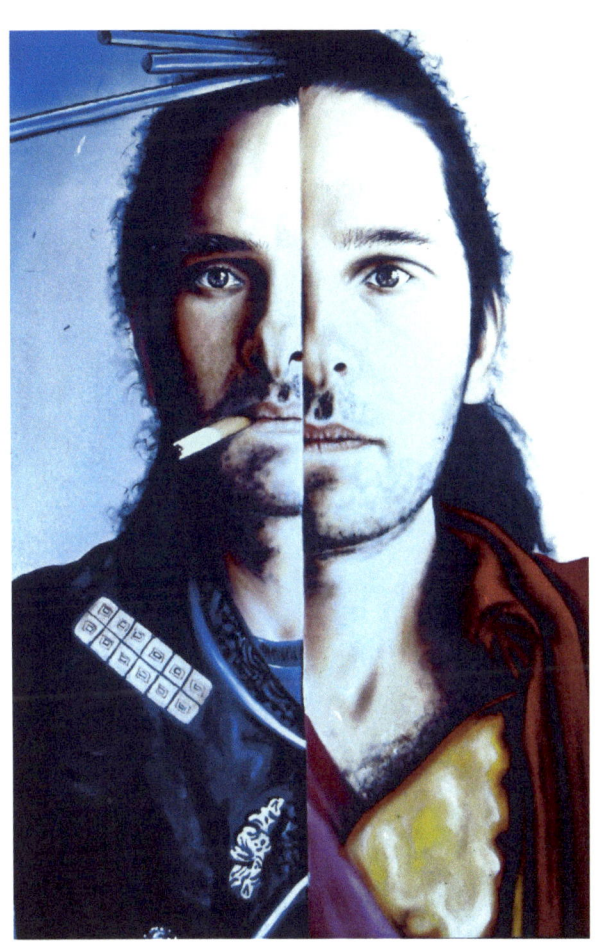

Disneyland, 2001, acrylic on canvas, 190 x 150 cm

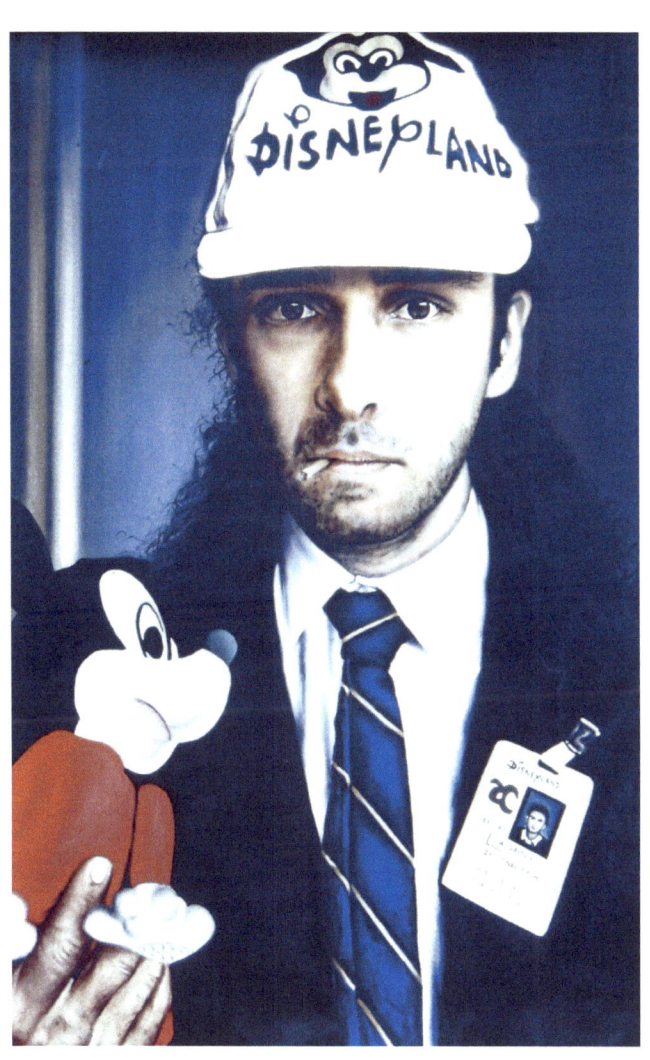

Raphrent, 2000, acrylic on canvas, 190 x 150 cm

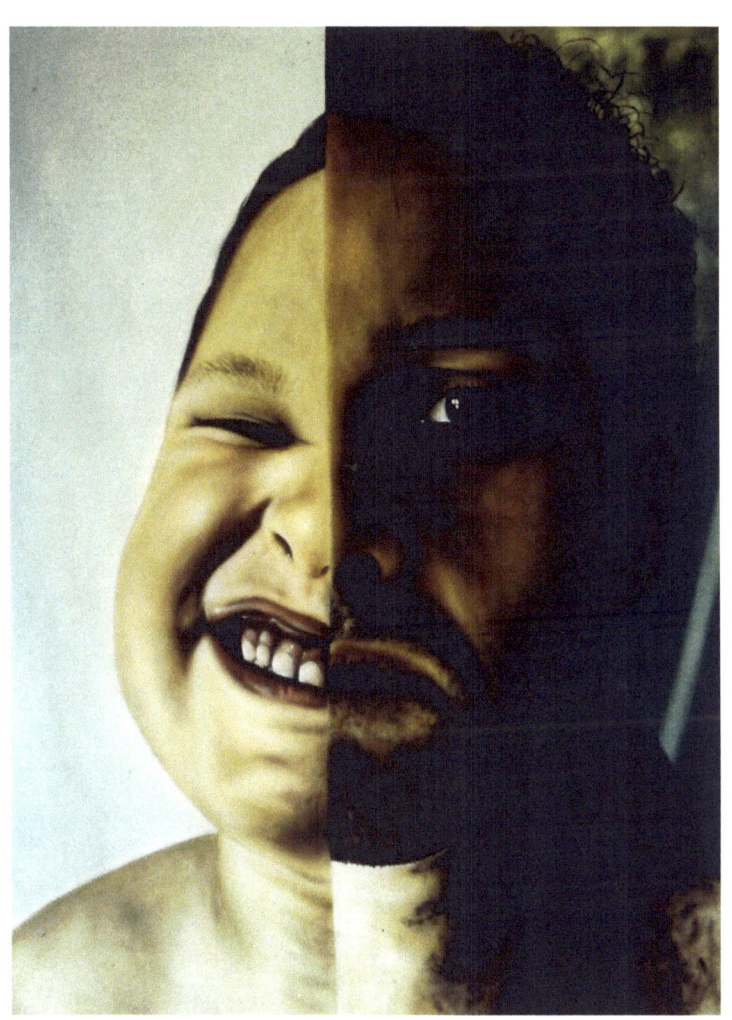

Can't you shave !, 2000, acrylic on canvas, 190 x 150 cm

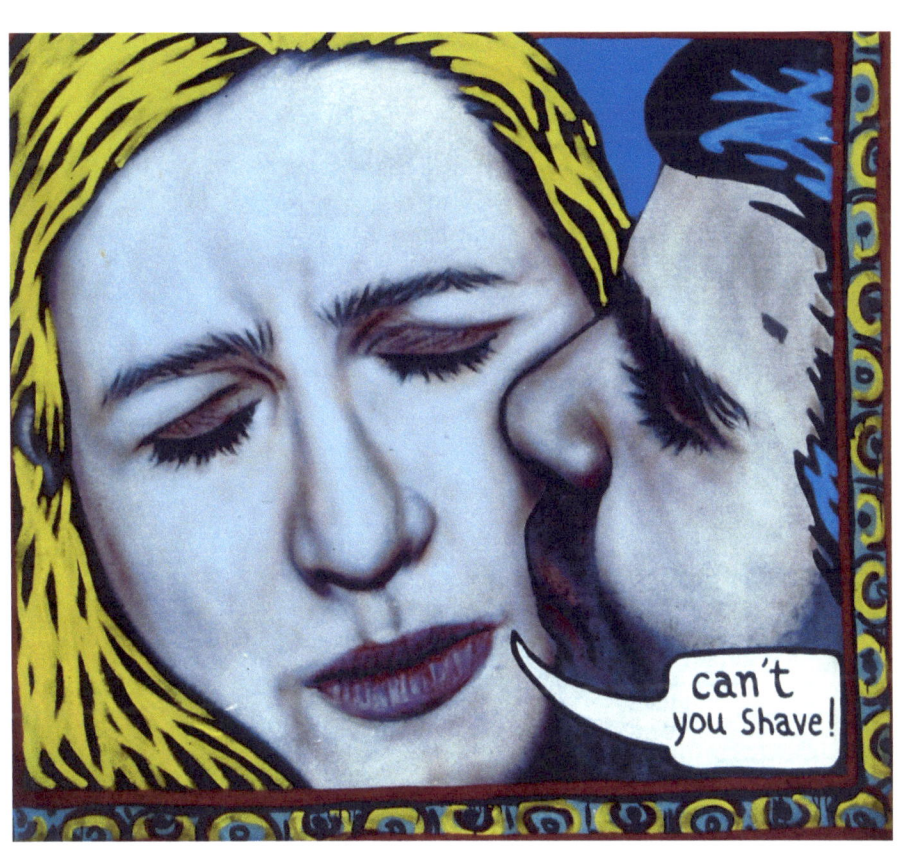

Self-portrait with Ray-Ban sunglasses, 2000, acrylic on canvas, 230 x 145 cm

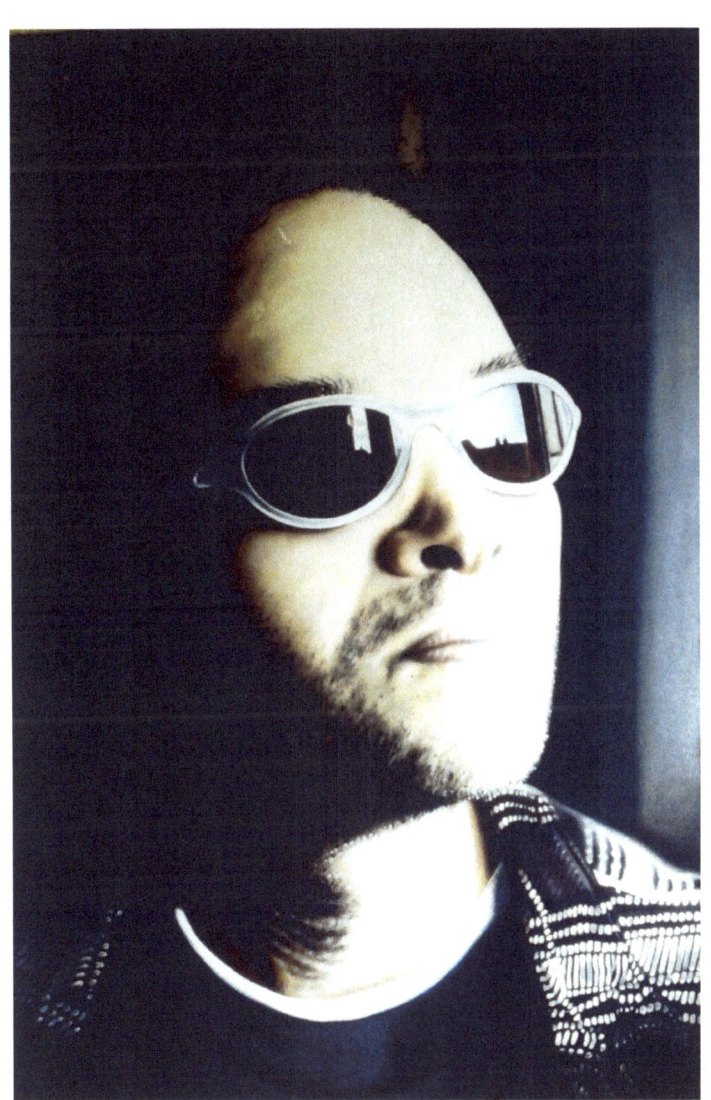

Chloë II, 2000, acrylic on canvas, 190 x 150 cm

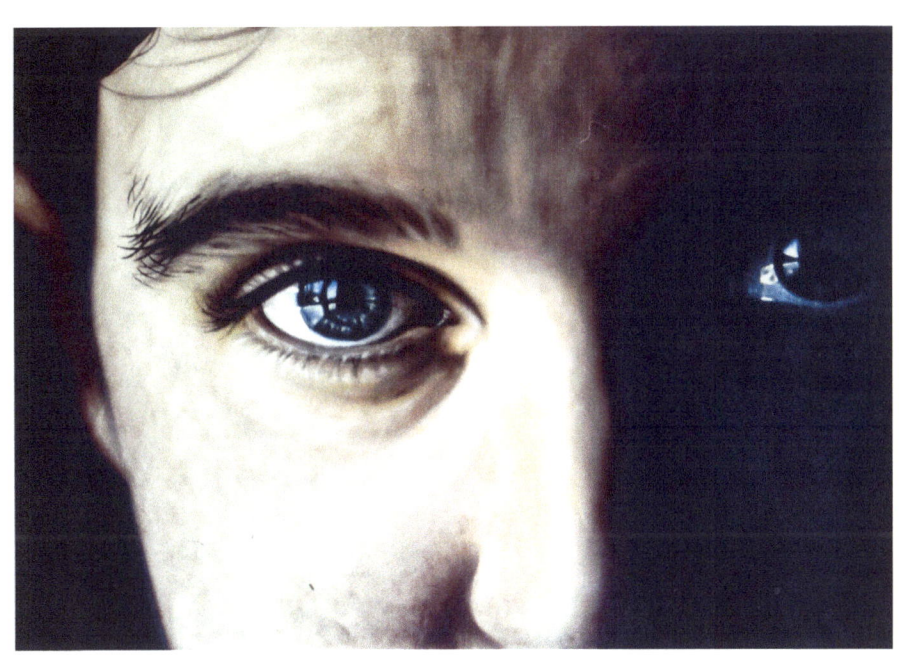

Greta I, 2000, acrylic on canvas, 200 x 150 cm

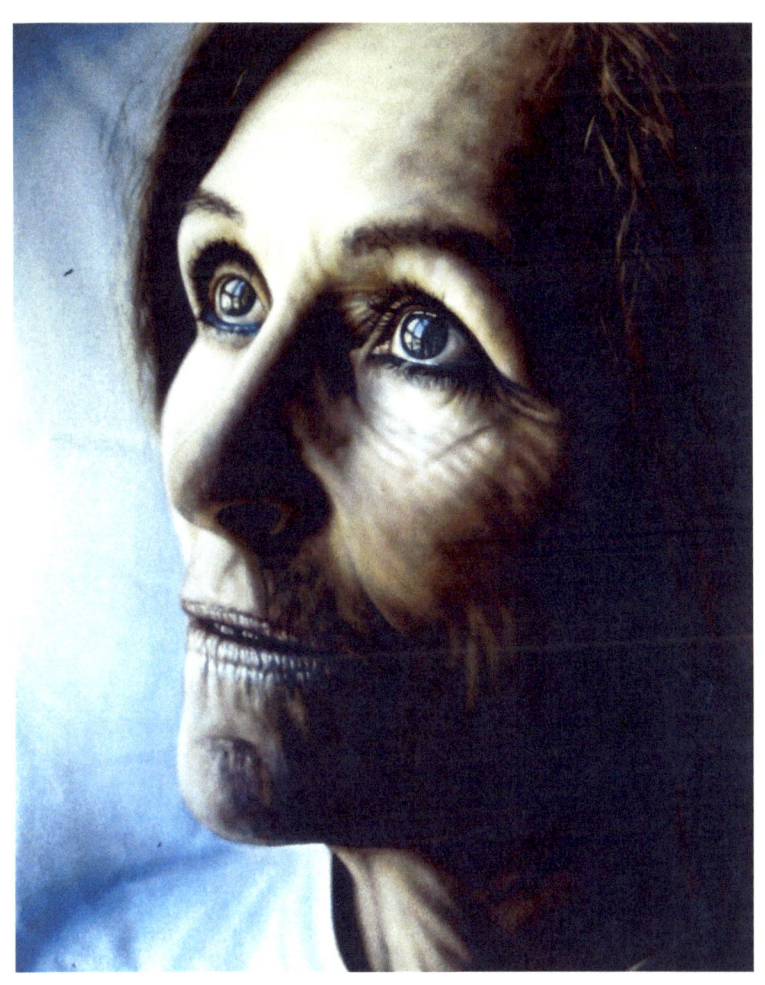

Gilles, 2001, acrylic on canvas, 240 x 150 cm

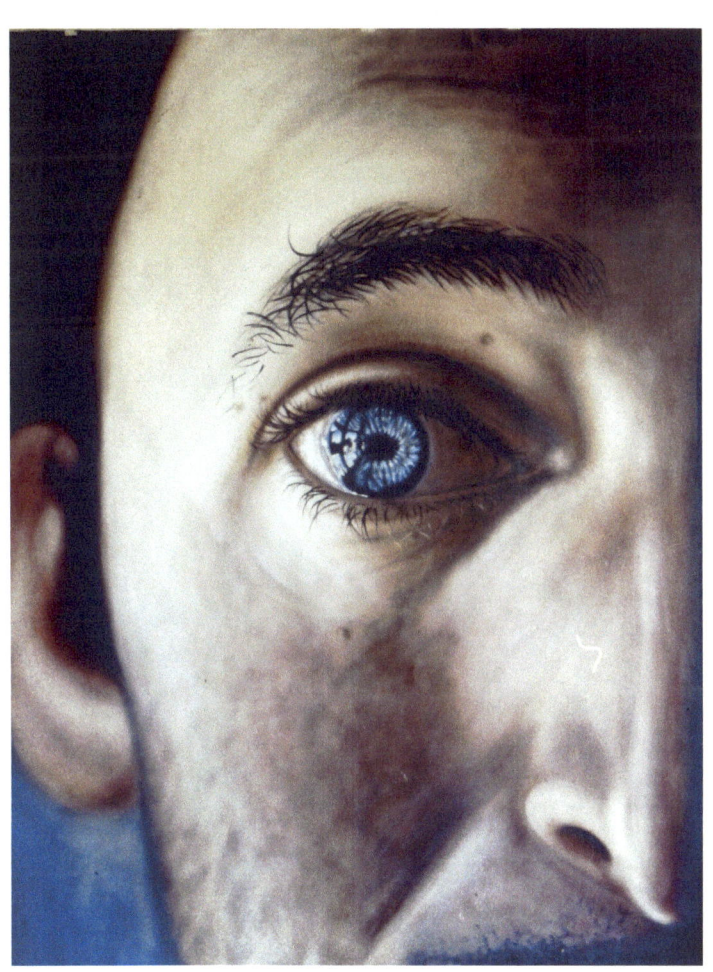

Greta II, 2000, acrylic on canvas, 190 x 150 cm

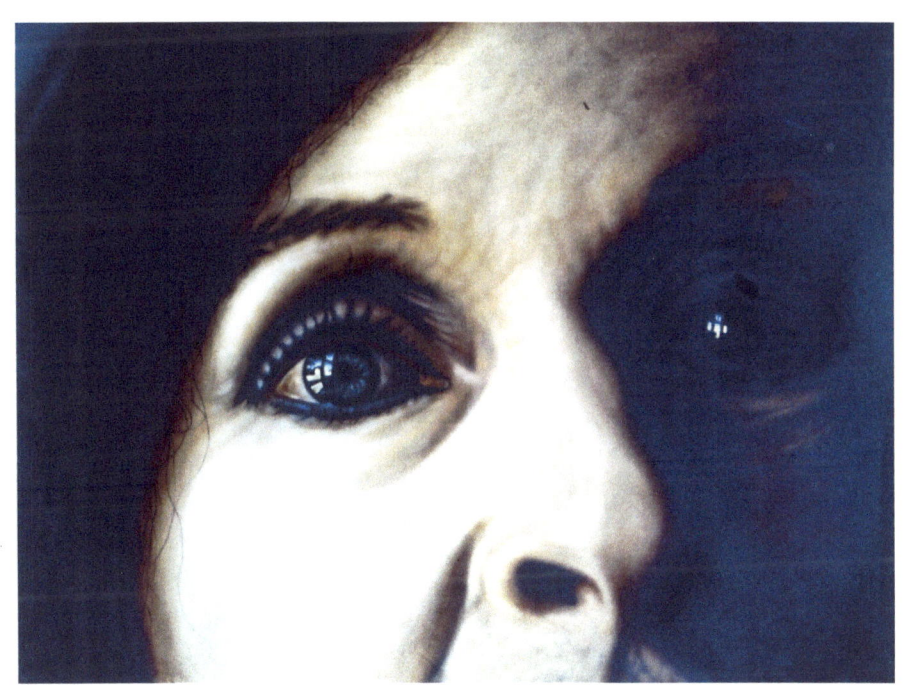

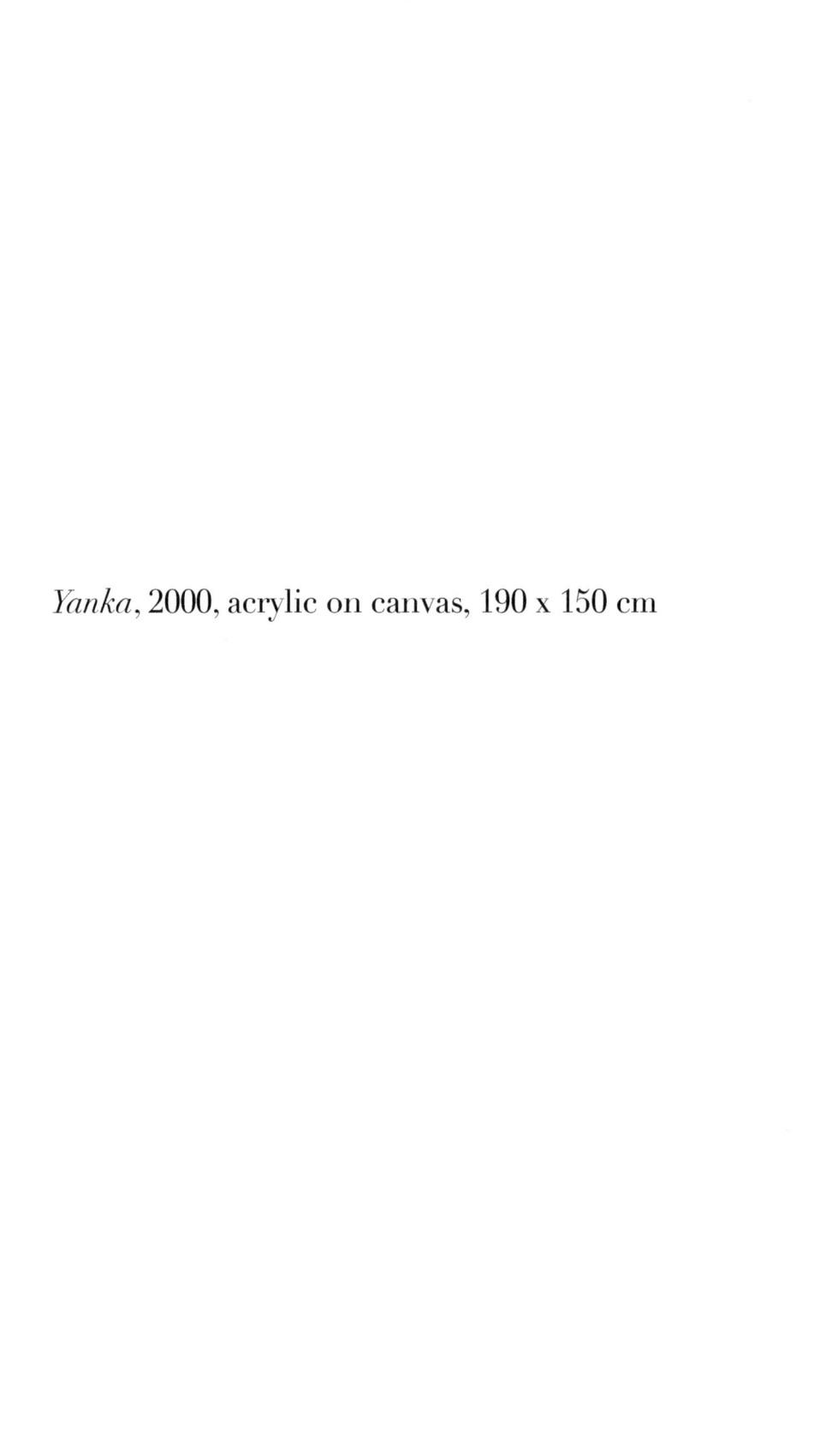

Yanka, 2000, acrylic on canvas, 190 x 150 cm

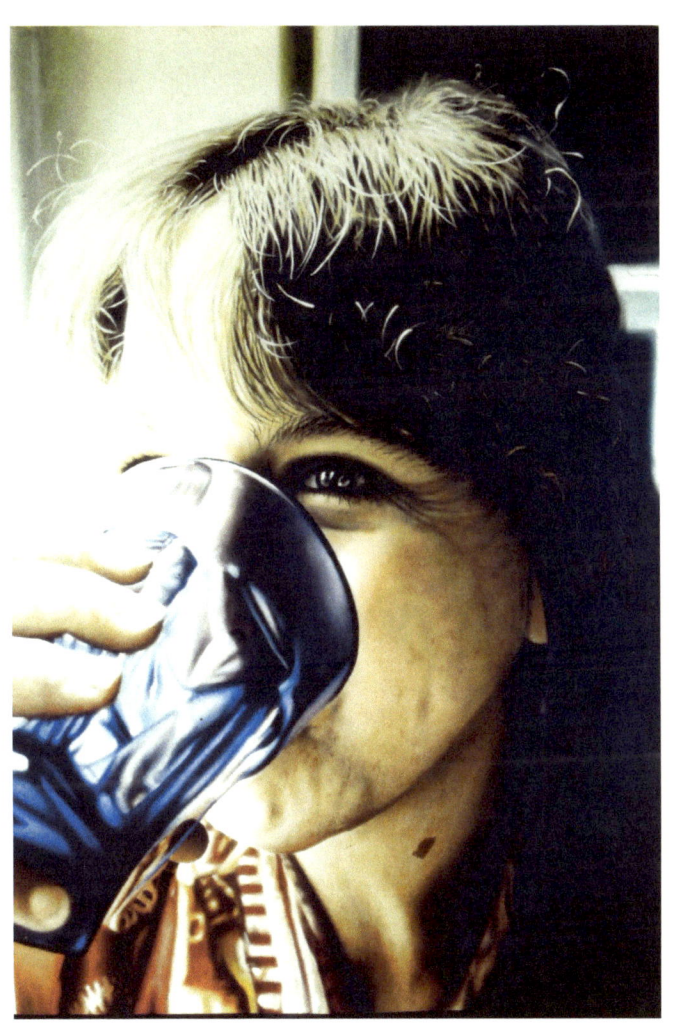

Chloë, 2000, acrylic on canvas, 250 x 180 cm

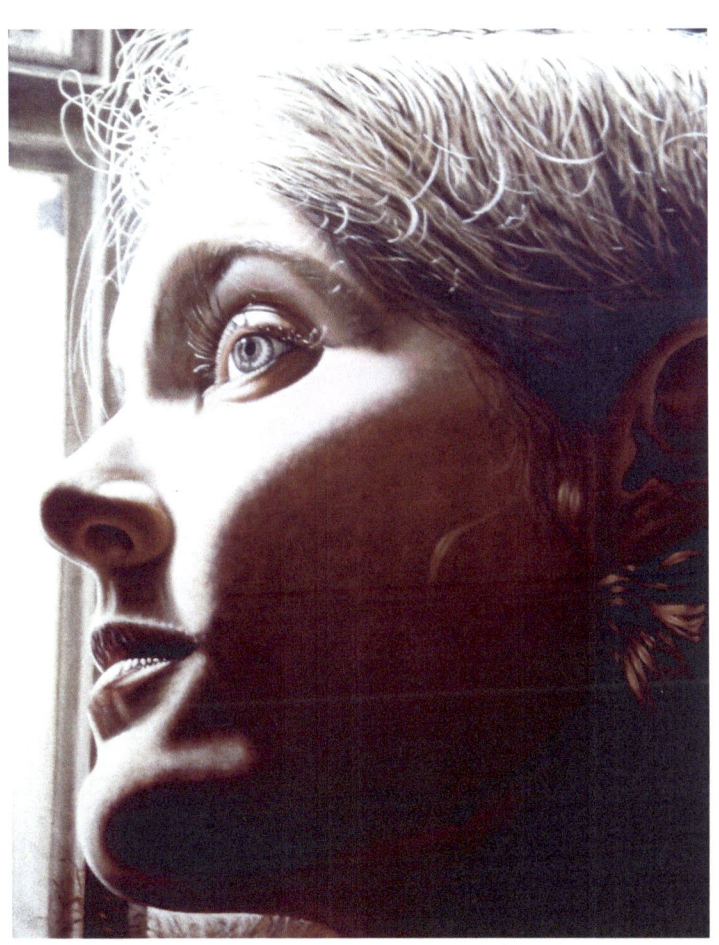

Marie, 2001, acrylic on canvas, 130 x 170 cm

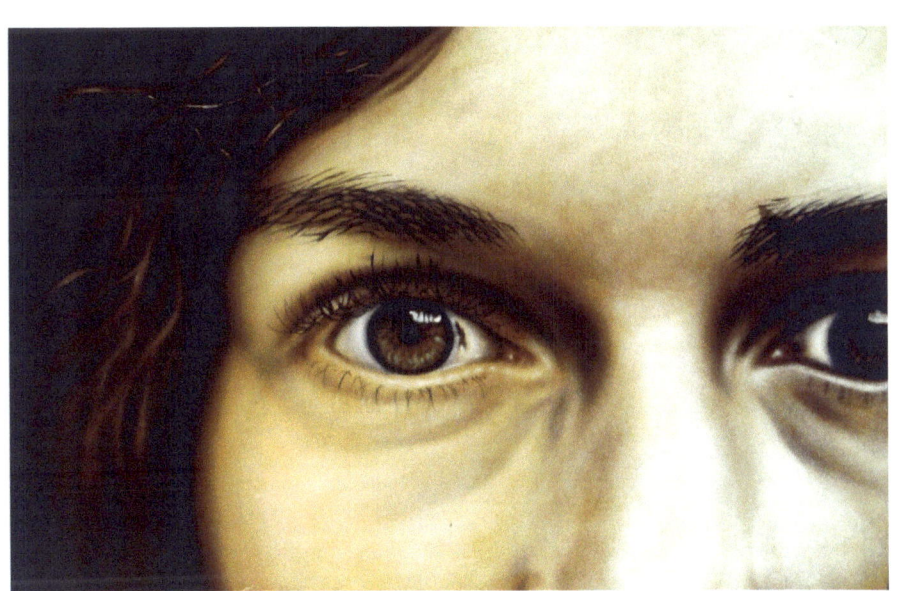

Self-portrait, *Untitled*, 2000, acrylic on canvas, 200 x 120 cm

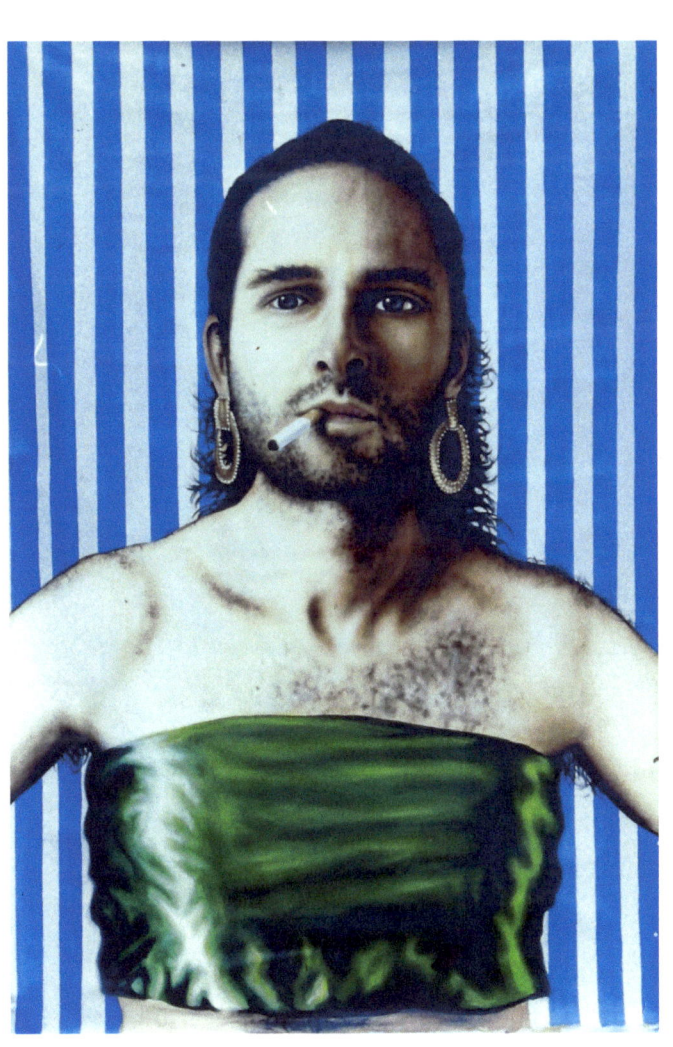

Chloë with sunglasses, 2000, acrylic on canvas, 190 x 150 cm

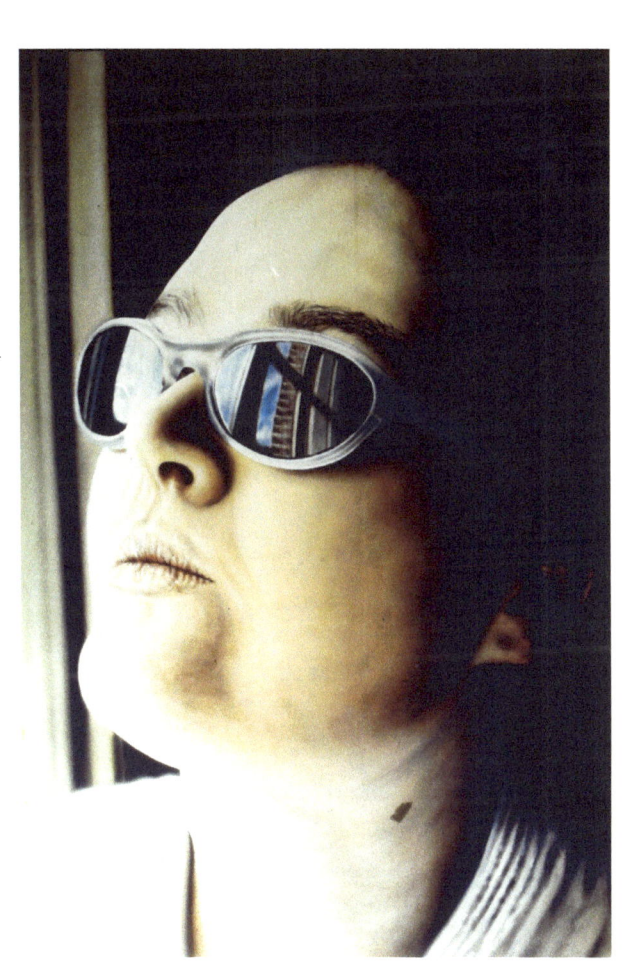

Figurative gradation of self-portrait with rasor and camera, 2001, acrylic on canvas, 195 x 145 cm

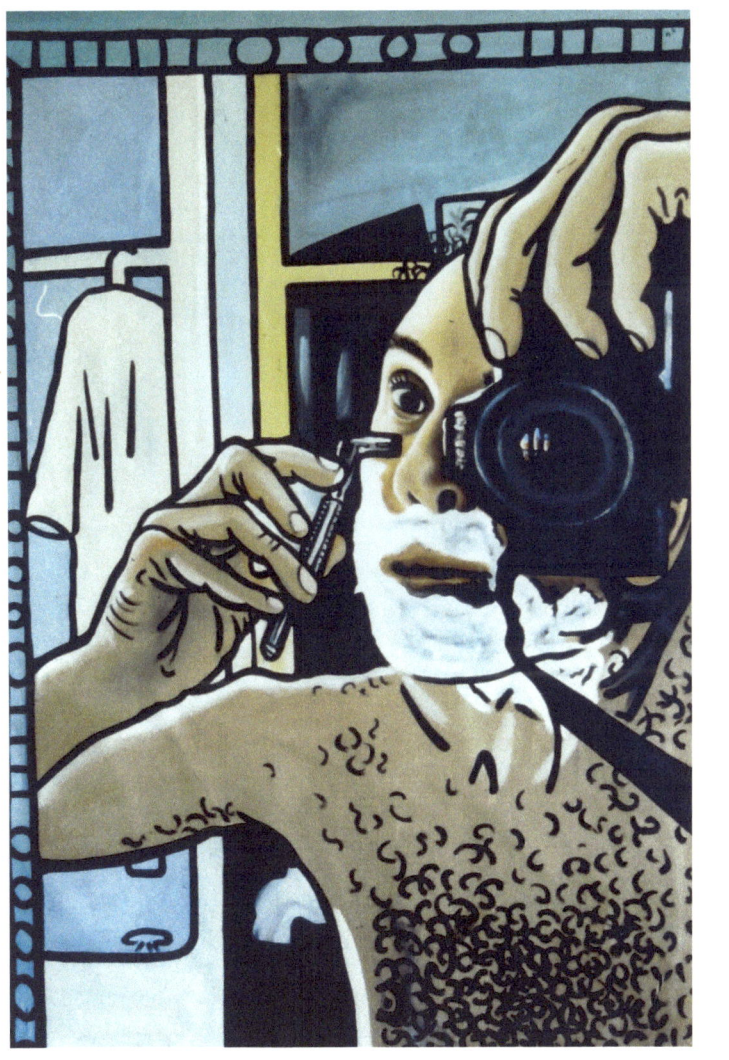

Contents

Choosing an identity: the Lama-Geisha, 2000, acrylic on canvas, 190 x 150 cm

Disneyland, 2001, acrylic on canvas, 190 x 150 cm

Raphrent, 2000, acrylic on canvas, 190 x 150 cm

Can't you shave !, 2000, acrylic on canvas, 190 x 150 cm

Self-portrait with Ray-Ban sunglasses, 2000, acrylic on canvas, 230 x 145 cm

Chloë II, 2000, acrylic on canvas, 190 x 150 cm

Greta I, 2000, acrylic on canvas, 200 x 150 cm

Gilles, 2001, acrylic on canvas, 240 x 150 cm

Greta II, 2000, acrylic on canvas, 190 x 150 cm

Yanka, 2000, acrylic on canvas, 190 x 150 cm

Chloë, 2000, acrylic on canvas, 250 x 180 cm

Marie, 2001, acrylic on canvas, 130 x 170 cm

Untitled, 2000, acrylic on canvas, 200 x 120 cm

Chloë with sunglasses, 2000, acrylic on canvas, 190 x 150 cm

Figurative gradation of self-portrait with rasor and camera, 2000, acrylic on canvas, 190 x 150 cm

About the artist

Laurent La Gamba was born on January 23rd, 1967, in Bondy, France.

After studying at the Sorbonne in Paris he travels abroad, staying for long periods of time in Los Angeles, California, in the United States.

His painting evolves hand in hand with photography: large canvases (using acrylic paint) which can be likened to American photorealism, he creates close-up portraits of his entourage, family and neighbours. In 1998-2001, he undertakes a series of caustic self-portraits, where cigarette dangling from his mouth, his face painted in a photorealist fashion he morphs into a stewardess, a Mc Donald's manager, Bob the Builder or a veiled woman. The focus is on the face, the background and accessories are painted with haste.

On his return to France he begins the first in situ series of camouflages and pro-cryptic installations (2002). He is working on these when he obtains a Pollock-Krasner Foundation grant and becomes artist-in-residence at La Napoule Art Foundation in Mandelieu. His work tilts into conceptual photography at this point.

While exploring the meaning of camouflage he creates painted installations for his static effigy. He dresses his models or himself in white suits which are then painted into a chosen environment so that they disappear. At first there are indoor portraits and then more elaborate outdoor portraits i.e. camouflage in supermarkets, airports, in front of cars, refrigerators, cookers etc.

Trained as a painter, Laurent La Gamba's photographs also rely on the aspect of performance.

Excerpts from psychoanalyst Jacques Lacan's writings often accompany the artist's work.

Laurent La Gamba
Works on canvas
Portraits and Self-portraits
1998 - 2001

ISBN: 978-1500758356

www.ingramcontent.com/pod-product-compliance
Lightning Source LLC
Chambersburg PA
CBHW040832180526
45159CB00001B/153